The Thrill of Money-Making:

Unleashing Your Inner Entrepreneur

By Marcus Edward Bond

Book Chapters:

1. The Power of a Money-Making Mindset
2. Identifying Your Unique Money-Making Skills and Talents
3. Turning Your Passion into Profit
4. Embracing Risk and Taking Action
5. Building a Strong Network of Business Relationships
6. The Importance of Marketing and Branding
7. Developing a Winning Sales Strategy
8. Harnessing the Power of Technology and Innovation
9. Scaling Your Business for Growth
10. Navigating Challenges and Overcoming Obstacles
11. The Role of Financial Planning in Money-Making
12. Investing in Your Future and Building Wealth
13. Giving Back and Making a Difference
14. Balancing Money-Making with Personal Fulfillment
15. The Thrill of Success: Celebrating Your Achievements

Book Introduction:

There's nothing quite like the thrill of making money. Whether you're an entrepreneur, investor, or simply looking to supplement your income, the art of money-making can be a deeply rewarding experience. In "The Thrill of Money-Making: Unleashing Your Inner Entrepreneur," we explore the emotional side of money-making and how to channel that energy into building a successful and fulfilling life.

Money-making is not just about making a quick buck. It's about tapping into your unique skills, talents, and passions and creating value in the world. It's about taking risks, embracing challenges, and learning from failures. It's about building strong relationships and leveraging technology to create innovative solutions to real-world problems. Most importantly, it's about finding personal fulfillment and making a difference in the world.

In this book, we'll explore the emotional journey of money-making and how to harness that energy to build a successful and fulfilling life. From developing a money-making mindset to identifying your unique skills and talents, to navigating challenges and obstacles, we'll provide you with the tools and strategies to unleash your inner entrepreneur and achieve your goals.

Chapter 1: The Power of a Money-Making Mindset

Money-making is not just about having the right skills or ideas. It's about having the right mindset. Your mindset is the foundation upon which your success is built. It determines your beliefs, attitudes, and behaviors, and ultimately, your results. In this chapter, we'll explore the power of a money-making mindset and how to develop one.

The first step in developing a money-making mindset is to believe that you can make money. Many people have limiting beliefs and negative attitudes about money, believing that it's either impossible or unethical to make money. This simply isn't true. Money is a tool that can be used to create value and make a difference in the world. By believing in your ability to make money, you open yourself up to new opportunities and possibilities.

The second step is to embrace risk and take action. Money-making requires taking calculated risks and stepping outside of your comfort zone. This can be scary, but it's necessary for growth and success. By taking action, you create momentum and move closer to your goals.

The third step is to cultivate a positive attitude and mindset. This means focusing on abundance rather than scarcity, embracing challenges and failures as opportunities for growth, and surrounding yourself with positive influences and mentors.

By developing a money-making mindset, you'll be able to approach money-making with confidence, passion, and a sense of purpose. In the next chapter, we'll explore how to identify your unique money-making skills and talents.

Identifying Your Unique Money-Making Skills and Talents

Chapter 2: Identifying Your Unique Money-Making Skills and Talents

Everyone has unique skills and talents that can be leveraged to make money. However, identifying those skills and talents can be a challenge. In this chapter, we'll explore how to uncover your unique money-making skills and talents and turn them into profitable ventures.

The first step in identifying your unique money-making skills and talents is to reflect on your passions and interests. What activities do you enjoy doing? What topics do you find yourself reading or learning about in your spare time? By exploring your passions and interests, you can identify areas where you have a natural aptitude and enthusiasm.

The second step is to assess your skills and experience. What skills have you developed over the years? What work experience or education do you have? By evaluating your skills and experience, you can identify areas where you have a competitive advantage and can provide value.

The third step is to solicit feedback from others. Ask your friends, family, and colleagues what they think your strengths are. You may be surprised to learn about skills or talents you didn't realize you had.

Once you've identified your unique money-making skills and talents, it's time to turn them into profitable ventures. This can be done by starting a business, offering freelance services, or creating a digital product or course. The key is to find a way to monetize your skills and talents in a way that is sustainable and profitable.

Identifying your unique money-making skills and talents can be a deeply fulfilling and emotional journey. It requires self-reflection, introspection, and a willingness to take a leap of faith. By tapping into your passions and talents, you can create a life that is both financially and personally fulfilling.

In the next chapter, we'll explore how to turn your passion into profit and create a business that aligns with your values and goals.

Embracing Risk and Taking Action

Chapter 4: Embracing Risk and Taking Action

Taking risks and stepping outside of your comfort zone is a critical component of money-making. However, it can be difficult to overcome the fear of failure and take that first step. In this chapter, we'll explore how to embrace risk and take action towards your money-making goals.

The first step in embracing risk is to acknowledge and accept that failure is a natural part of the process. Every successful money-making venture involves some degree of risk and failure. It's important to view failure as an opportunity for growth and learning, rather than a reflection of your worth or abilities.

The second step is to develop a plan and take action. Procrastination and indecision can paralyze you and prevent you from taking the necessary steps towards your goals. By creating a plan and taking action, you create momentum and build confidence.

The third step is to seek out support and guidance. Money-making can be a lonely journey, but it doesn't have to be. Surrounding yourself with supportive and knowledgeable individuals can provide you with the encouragement and resources you need to succeed.

Embracing risk and taking action towards your money-making goals can be a deeply emotional and empowering experience. It requires courage, determination, and a willingness to face uncertainty. However, the rewards of taking action towards your goals can be life-changing.

In the next chapter, we'll explore how to build a strong network of business relationships and leverage those relationships to grow your money-making ventures.

Chapter 5: Building a Strong Network of Business Relationships

Building a strong network of business relationships is essential for success in money-making. The right connections can provide you with valuable insights, opportunities, and resources. However, building relationships can be a challenging and emotional process. In this chapter, we'll explore how to build a strong network of business relationships and leverage those relationships to grow your money-making ventures.

The first step in building a strong network of business relationships is to focus on providing value to others. People are more likely to want to build a relationship with you if they feel that you can provide them with something of value. This can be in the form of advice, resources, or connections.

The second step is to be genuine and authentic in your interactions. People can sense when you are being insincere or inauthentic. By being yourself and showing a genuine interest in others, you can build trust and establish meaningful connections.

The third step is to be proactive in seeking out connections and opportunities. Attend networking events, join online communities, and reach out to individuals who inspire you or have skills and expertise that you can learn from.

Building a strong network of business relationships can be a deeply emotional and rewarding experience. It requires vulnerability, empathy, and a willingness to invest time and energy in others. However, the rewards of building strong connections can be immense.

Once you've built a strong network of business relationships, it's important to leverage those relationships to grow your money-making ventures. This can be done by collaborating on projects, sharing resources, or referring each other to potential clients or customers.

In the next chapter, we'll explore the importance of marketing and branding in money-making and how to develop a winning marketing strategy.

The Importance of Marketing and Branding

Chapter 6: The Importance of Marketing and Branding

Marketing and branding are essential components of money-making. They are the tools that enable you to reach your target audience, establish your brand identity, and communicate the value of your products or services. In this chapter, we'll explore the emotional side of marketing and branding and how to develop a winning marketing strategy.

The first step in developing a winning marketing strategy is to identify your target audience. Who are your ideal customers or clients? What are their needs and desires? By understanding your target audience, you can create marketing messages that resonate with them and address their pain points.

The second step is to establish your brand identity. Your brand identity is the unique personality and image that you want to convey to your target audience. It should reflect your values, mission, and vision. Your brand identity should be consistent across all marketing channels, including your website, social media, and advertising.

The third step is to develop a marketing plan that aligns with your goals and resources. This may include social media marketing, email marketing, content marketing, or paid advertising. The key is to focus on channels that will enable you to reach your target audience and communicate the value of your products or services.

Marketing and branding can be a deeply emotional and personal journey. It requires a deep understanding of your target audience and a willingness to be vulnerable and authentic in your communication. However, the rewards of effective marketing and branding can be immense, including increased brand awareness, customer loyalty, and revenue.

In the next chapter, we'll explore how to develop a winning sales strategy and close more deals

The Importance of Marketing and Branding

Chapter 6: The Importance of Marketing and Branding

Marketing and branding are the lifeblood of money-making. They are the tools that enable you to showcase your unique value proposition, differentiate yourself from the competition, and connect with your ideal customers. In this chapter, we'll explore the emotional side of marketing and branding and how to develop a winning marketing strategy.

The first step in developing a winning marketing strategy is to identify your ideal customer. Who are they? What are their needs and desires? By understanding your ideal customer, you can create marketing messages that speak directly to them and build a connection based on mutual understanding.

The second step is to establish your brand identity. Your brand identity is the essence of who you are and what you stand for. It should reflect your values, mission, and vision. Your brand identity should be consistent across all marketing channels, including your website, social media, and advertising.

The third step is to develop a marketing plan that aligns with your goals and resources. This may include social media marketing, email marketing, content marketing, or paid advertising. The key is to focus on channels that will enable you to reach your ideal customer and showcase your unique value proposition.

Marketing and branding can be an emotional journey, full of highs and lows. It requires a deep understanding of your target audience, a willingness to be vulnerable and authentic in your communication, and the ability to adapt to changing market conditions. However, the rewards of effective marketing and branding can be immense, including increased brand awareness, customer loyalty, and revenue.

In the next chapter, we'll explore how to develop a winning sales strategy and close more deals.

Developing a Winning Sales Strategy

Chapter 7: Developing a Winning Sales Strategy

Sales are the lifeblood of money-making. They are the means by which you convert leads into paying customers and generate revenue for your business. In this chapter, we'll explore the emotional side of sales and how to develop a winning sales strategy that resonates with your ideal customer.

The first step in developing a winning sales strategy is to understand your ideal customer's pain points. What challenges do they face? What are their goals and aspirations? By understanding their pain points, you can position your product or service as the solution they need.

The second step is to establish trust and build a relationship with your ideal customer. People are more likely to buy from someone they trust and feel a connection with. This can be done through personalization, empathy, and active listening.

The third step is to communicate the value of your product or service in a way that resonates with your ideal customer. This may involve highlighting the benefits, addressing objections, and providing social proof.

Developing a winning sales strategy can be an emotional journey, full of highs and lows. It requires a deep understanding of your ideal customer, a willingness to be vulnerable and authentic in your communication, and the ability to adapt to changing market conditions. However, the rewards of a winning sales strategy can be immense, including increased revenue, customer loyalty, and personal fulfillment.

In the next chapter, we'll explore how to harness the power of technology and innovation to grow your money-making ventures.

Harnessing the Power of Technology and Innovation

Chapter 8: Harnessing the Power of Technology and Innovation

Technology and innovation are game-changers in money-making. They have the power to automate processes, increase efficiency, and reach new customers. In this chapter, we'll explore the emotional side of technology and innovation and how to harness their power to grow your money-making ventures.

The first step in harnessing the power of technology and innovation is to stay up-to-date with the latest trends and developments. This may involve attending industry events, reading industry publications, and networking with other professionals in your field.

The second step is to identify areas where technology and innovation can be leveraged to improve your business processes or create new revenue streams. This may involve implementing new software or tools, developing new products or services, or exploring new marketing channels.

The third step is to embrace experimentation and risk-taking. Technology and innovation are inherently uncertain, and not every new initiative will be successful. However, by embracing experimentation and learning from failures, you can create a culture of innovation that drives growth and success.

Harnessing the power of technology and innovation can be a deeply emotional and exciting journey. It requires a willingness to embrace change, take risks, and invest in the future. However, the rewards of harnessing the power of technology and innovation can be immense, including increased revenue, customer satisfaction, and personal fulfillment.

In the next chapter, we'll explore how to build a strong team and cultivate a culture of success that drives your money-making ventures forward.

Scaling Your Business for Growth

Chapter 9: Scaling Your Business for Growth

Scaling your business for growth can be one of the most emotional and exhilarating experiences in money-making. It requires a willingness to take risks, make tough decisions, and embrace change. In this chapter, we'll explore how to scale your business for growth and achieve your money-making goals.

The first step in scaling your business for growth is to assess your current business model and identify areas where improvement or expansion is possible. This may involve exploring new products or services, entering new markets, or developing new marketing channels.

The second step is to develop a growth plan that aligns with your long-term vision and goals. This may involve setting targets, identifying key performance indicators, and outlining specific action steps to achieve your growth goals.

The third step is to build a strong team and cultivate a culture of success. Scaling your business requires a team of talented and motivated individuals who share your vision and values. It's important to invest in your team and provide them with the resources and support they need to succeed.

Scaling your business for growth can be a deeply emotional journey, full of excitement, anxiety, and uncertainty. It requires a willingness to take risks, make tough decisions, and embrace change. However, the rewards of scaling your business for growth can be immense, including increased revenue, market share, and personal fulfillment.

In the next chapter, we'll explore how to navigate the ups and downs of money-making and maintain a resilient mindset that enables you to thrive in the face of adversity.

Navigating Challenges and Overcoming Obstacles

Chapter 10: Navigating Challenges and Overcoming Obstacles

Navigating challenges and overcoming obstacles is an inevitable part of money-making. It can be emotionally draining, but it's essential for growth and success. In this chapter, we'll explore how to navigate challenges and overcome obstacles, while maintaining a resilient mindset that enables you to thrive in the face of adversity.

The first step in navigating challenges and overcoming obstacles is to accept that setbacks are a natural part of the money-making process. It's important to view challenges as opportunities for growth and learning, rather than failures.

The second step is to stay focused on your long-term goals and vision. It's easy to get sidetracked by short-term setbacks or distractions. By staying focused on your long-term goals, you can maintain the motivation and perseverance needed to overcome obstacles.

The third step is to seek out support and guidance when you need it. Money-making can be a lonely journey, but it doesn't have to be. Surrounding yourself with supportive and knowledgeable individuals can provide you with the encouragement and resources you need to overcome obstacles.

Navigating challenges and overcoming obstacles can be a deeply emotional and draining experience. It requires a resilient mindset, a willingness to embrace discomfort and uncertainty, and the ability to adapt to changing circumstances. However, the rewards of overcoming obstacles can be immense, including increased confidence, resilience, and personal growth.

In the next chapter, we'll explore how to manage your finances effectively and make smart investments that support your money-making goals.

The Role of Financial Planning in Money-Making

Chapter 11: The Role of Financial Planning in Money-Making

Financial planning is an essential component of money-making. It's the foundation upon which you build your money-making ventures, and it provides the structure and guidance needed to achieve your financial goals. In this chapter, we'll explore the emotional side of financial planning and how to make smart investments that support your money-making goals.

The first step in effective financial planning is to set clear financial goals that align with your long-term vision and values. This may involve identifying your current financial position, assessing your risk tolerance, and establishing a plan for achieving your financial goals.

The second step is to develop a budget and track your spending. This can be a difficult and emotional process, but it's essential for understanding where your money is going and making necessary adjustments.

The third step is to make smart investments that support your money-making goals. This may involve investing in your own education and development, or investing in assets that generate passive income.

Financial planning can be an emotional journey, full of highs and lows. It requires discipline, patience, and a willingness to make tough decisions. However, the rewards of effective financial planning can be immense, including financial freedom, stability, and security.

In the next chapter, we'll explore the importance of continuous learning and personal development in money-making, and how to stay ahead of the curve in a rapidly changing business landscape.

Investing in Your Future and Building Wealth

Chapter 12: Investing in Your Future and Building Wealth

Investing in your future and building wealth is the ultimate goal of money-making. It's the culmination of all your hard work and dedication, and it provides the foundation for financial freedom and security. In this chapter, we'll explore the emotional side of investing and how to build wealth through smart financial decisions.

The first step in building wealth is to understand the importance of saving and investing. It's easy to get caught up in short-term gratification, but the long-term benefits of saving and investing are immense.

The second step is to develop a long-term investment strategy that aligns with your goals and values. This may involve diversifying your portfolio, investing in stocks, real estate, or other assets, and regularly reviewing and adjusting your strategy as needed.

The third step is to cultivate a mindset of abundance and prosperity. It's important to believe that you can achieve your financial goals and that there are abundant opportunities available to you.

Building wealth can be an emotional journey, full of uncertainty and risk. It requires discipline, patience, and a willingness to make tough decisions. However, the rewards of building wealth can be immense, including financial freedom, stability, and security.

In the next chapter, we'll explore the importance of giving back and making a positive impact on the world through your money-making ventures.

Chapter 13: Giving Back and Making a Difference

Money-making is not just about personal gain and financial success. It's also about making a positive impact on the world and giving back to the community. In this chapter, we'll explore the emotional side of giving back and making a difference through your money-making ventures.

The first step in making a positive impact is to identify causes or issues that align with your values and mission. This may involve supporting local charities, donating a portion of your profits to a specific cause, or volunteering your time and resources.

The second step is to incorporate social responsibility into your business model. This may involve implementing environmentally-friendly practices, promoting social justice, or creating products or services that benefit society as a whole.

The third step is to cultivate a mindset of generosity and empathy. It's important to remember that money-making is not just about personal gain, but about using your resources to create a better world for everyone.

Giving back and making a difference can be an emotional journey, full of joy, empathy, and gratitude. It requires a willingness to be vulnerable, empathetic, and to see the world beyond your own needs and desires. However, the rewards of giving back and making a difference can be immense, including personal fulfillment, community impact, and social change.

In the next chapter, we'll explore the importance of work-life balance and self-care in money-making, and how to maintain a healthy and fulfilling life outside of work.

Balancing Money-Making with Personal Fulfillment

Chapter 14: Balancing Money-Making with Personal Fulfillment

Money-making can be an all-consuming endeavor, but it's important to remember the value of personal fulfillment and work-life balance. In this chapter, we'll explore the emotional side of balancing money-making with personal fulfillment, and how to create a life that is both financially and personally fulfilling.

The first step in balancing money-making with personal fulfillment is to identify your values and priorities. This may involve assessing your personal and professional goals, and developing a plan to achieve them.

The second step is to establish boundaries and carve out time for self-care and personal pursuits. This may involve scheduling time for exercise, hobbies, or time with loved ones.

The third step is to cultivate a mindset of gratitude and appreciation. It's important to remember the value of the experiences and relationships that bring joy and meaning to your life.

Balancing money-making with personal fulfillment can be an emotional journey, full of introspection, reflection, and vulnerability. It requires a willingness to acknowledge and address the emotional toll of work and money-making, and to prioritize personal growth and happiness.

In the final chapter, we'll explore the importance of maintaining a long-term perspective in money-making, and how to ensure sustainable success over time.

The Thrill of Success: Celebrating Your Achievements

Chapter 15: The Thrill of Success: Celebrating Your Achievements

Money-making is a journey full of challenges and triumphs. It's important to celebrate your achievements along the way and acknowledge the hard work and dedication that led to your success. In this chapter, we'll explore the emotional side of success and how to celebrate your achievements in a meaningful and fulfilling way.

The first step in celebrating your achievements is to acknowledge the hard work and dedication that led to your success. It's important to take time to reflect on the challenges you faced and the obstacles you overcame to achieve your goals.

The second step is to celebrate your achievements in a way that is meaningful and fulfilling to you. This may involve sharing your success with loved ones, treating yourself to a special gift or experience, or taking time to reflect on the impact of your achievements.

The third step is to maintain a mindset of gratitude and humility. It's important to remember that success is not just about personal gain, but about creating a positive impact on the world.

Celebrating your achievements can be an emotional journey, full of joy, pride, and gratitude. It requires a willingness to acknowledge and celebrate your successes, and to use them as inspiration for future growth and achievement.

In conclusion, money-making is a journey full of emotional highs and lows. It requires discipline, perseverance, and a willingness to embrace risk and uncertainty. By cultivating a mindset of resilience, gratitude, and abundance, you can achieve your money-making goals and create a life that is both financially and personally fulfilling.

Some more monkey making books to explore

100 Money-Making Books That Will Inspire and Empower You

Money-making is a complex and multifaceted journey, full of challenges and triumphs. Fortunately, there are countless books that can help inspire and empower you along the way. In this list, we've compiled 100 of the best money-making books that can help you achieve your financial goals and create a life that is both financially and personally fulfilling.

1. Rich Dad Poor Dad by Robert Kiyosaki
2. The Millionaire Next Door by Thomas J. Stanley and William D. Danko
3. The 4-Hour Work Week by Timothy Ferriss
4. The Richest Man in Babylon by George S. Clason
5. Think and Grow Rich by Napoleon Hill
6. The Total Money Makeover by Dave Ramsey
7. The Automatic Millionaire by David Bach
8. The Psychology of Money by Morgan Housel
9. The Compound Effect by Darren Hardy
10. The Lean Startup by Eric Ries
11. The E-Myth Revisited by Michael E. Gerber
12. The 7 Habits of Highly Effective People by Stephen Covey
13. The One Thing by Gary Keller and Jay Papasan
14. The Power of Habit by Charles Duhigg
15. The 10X Rule by Grant Cardone
16. The Art of Possibility by Rosamund Stone Zander and Benjamin Zander
17. The Alchemist by Paulo Coelho
18. The Innovator's Dilemma by Clayton M. Christensen
19. The Hard Thing About Hard Things by Ben Horowitz
20. The 80/20 Principle by Richard Koch
21. The Millionaire Fastlane by MJ DeMarco
22. The Intelligent Investor by Benjamin Graham
23. The Simple Path to Wealth by JL Collins
24. The Go-Giver by Bob Burg and John David Mann
25. The War of Art by Steven Pressfield
26. The Millionaire Mind by Thomas J. Stanley
27. The Science of Getting Rich by Wallace D. Wattles
28. The Law of Success by Napoleon Hill
29. The Big Leap by Gay Hendricks
30. The Wealth of Nations by Adam Smith
31. The Strangest Secret by Earl Nightingale
32. The 5 AM Club by Robin Sharma
33. The Art of Non-Conformity by Chris Guillebeau
34. The Power of Positive Thinking by Norman Vincent Peale
35. The Wealthy Barber by David Chilton
36. The Compound Effect by Darren Hardy
37. The Millionaire Messenger by Brendon Burchard

38. The Millionaire Real Estate Agent by Gary Keller
39. The Psychology of Selling by Brian Tracy
40. The Psychology of Achievement by Brian Tracy
41. The Business of the 21st Century by Robert T. Kiyosaki
42. The Automatic Customer by John Warrillow
43. The Lean Entrepreneur by Brant Cooper and Patrick Vlaskovits
44. The Personal MBA by Josh Kaufman
45. The Lean Product Playbook by Dan Olsen
46. The Lean Analytics by Alistair Croll and Benjamin Yoskovitz
47. The Innovator's Solution by Clayton M. Christensen and Michael E. Raynor
48. The Hard Thing About Hard Things by Ben Horowitz
49. The Lean Product Development Guidebook by Ronald Mascitelli
50. The Lean Startup by Eric Ries
51. The One Minute Manager by Kenneth H. Blanchard and Spencer Johnson
52. The 5 Elements of Effective Thinking by Edward B. Burger and Michael Starbird
53. The Art of Learning by Josh Waitzkin

Here are another 45 inspiring money-making books that can help you achieve your financial goals and live a fulfilling life:

1. The Millionaire Next Door by Thomas J. Stanley and William D. Danko
2. The 4-Hour Work Week by Timothy Ferriss
3. The Richest Man in Babylon by George S. Clason
4. Think and Grow Rich by Napoleon Hill
5. The Total Money Makeover by Dave Ramsey
6. The Automatic Millionaire by David Bach
7. The Psychology of Money by Morgan Housel
8. The Compound Effect by Darren Hardy
9. The Lean Startup by Eric Ries
10. The E-Myth Revisited by Michael E. Gerber
11. The 7 Habits of Highly Effective People by Stephen Covey
12. The One Thing by Gary Keller and Jay Papasan
13. The Power of Habit by Charles Duhigg
14. The 10X Rule by Grant Cardone
15. The Art of Possibility by Rosamund Stone Zander and Benjamin Zander
16. The Alchemist by Paulo Coelho
17. The Innovator's Dilemma by Clayton M. Christensen
18. The Hard Thing About Hard Things by Ben Horowitz
19. The 80/20 Principle by Richard Koch
20. The Millionaire Fastlane by MJ DeMarco
21. The Intelligent Investor by Benjamin Graham
22. The Simple Path to Wealth by JL Collins
23. The Go-Giver by Bob Burg and John David Mann
24. The War of Art by Steven Pressfield
25. The Millionaire Mind by Thomas J. Stanley
26. The Science of Getting Rich by Wallace D. Wattles
27. The Law of Success by Napoleon Hill
28. The Big Leap by Gay Hendricks
29. The Wealth of Nations by Adam Smith

30. The Strangest Secret by Earl Nightingale
31. The 5 AM Club by Robin Sharma
32. The Art of Non-Conformity by Chris Guillebeau
33. The Power of Positive Thinking by Norman Vincent Peale
34. The Wealthy Barber by David Chilton
35. The Compound Effect by Darren Hardy
36. The Millionaire Messenger by Brendon Burchard
37. The Millionaire Real Estate Agent by Gary Keller
38. The Psychology of Selling by Brian Tracy
39. The Psychology of Achievement by Brian Tracy
40. The Business of the 21st Century by Robert T. Kiyosaki
41. The Automatic Customer by John Warrillow
42. The Lean Entrepreneur by Brant Cooper and Patrick Vlaskovits
43. The Personal MBA by Josh Kaufman
44. The Lean Product Playbook by Dan Olsen
45. The Lean Analytics by Alistair Croll and Benjamin Yoskovitz

These books cover a range of topics, including personal finance, entrepreneurship, investing, and mindset. Reading them can help you gain valuable insights, develop new skills, and stay motivated on your money-making journey.